Donated by

ROTARY CLUB
OF WEST CHESTER
2008

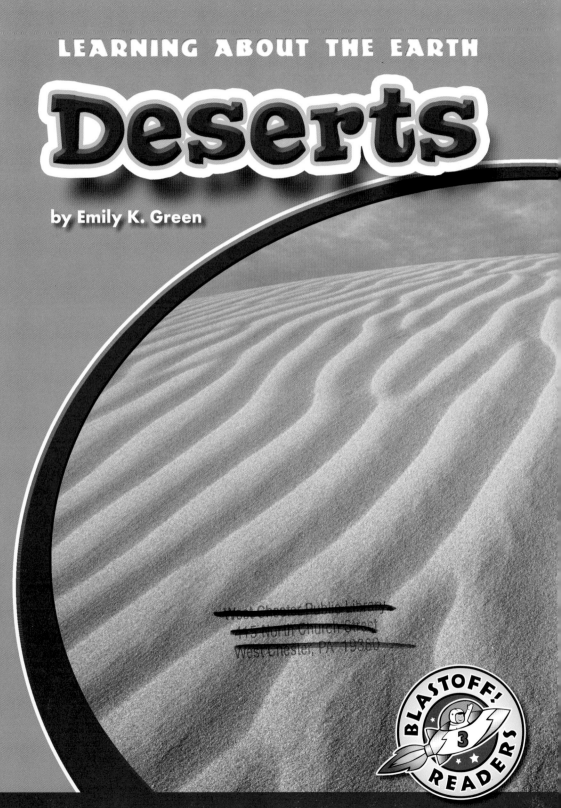

LEARNING ABOUT THE EARTH

Deserts

by Emily K. Green

BLASTOFF!
3
READERS

BELLWETHER MEDIA · MINNEAPOLIS, MN

Note to Librarians, Teachers, and Parents:

Blastoff! Readers are carefully developed by literacy experts and combine standards-based content with developmentally appropriate text.

Level 1 provides the most support through repetition of high-frequency words, light text, predictable sentence patterns, and strong visual support.

Level 2 offers early readers a bit more challenge through varied simple sentences, increased text load, and less repetition of high-frequency words.

Level 3 advances early-fluent readers toward fluency through increased text and concept load, less reliance on visuals, longer sentences, and more literary language.

Whichever book is right for your reader, Blastoff! Readers are the perfect books to build confidence and encourage a love of reading that will last a lifetime!

This edition first published in 2007 by Bellwether Media.

No part of this publication may be reproduced in whole or in part without written permission of the publisher. For information regarding permission, write to Bellwether Media Inc., Attention: Permissions Department, Post Office Box 1C, Minnetonka, MN 55345-9998.

Library of Congress Cataloging-in-Publication Data
Green, Emily K., 1966–
  Deserts / by Emily K. Green.
    p. cm. – (Blastoff! readers) (Learning about the Earth)
Summary: "Simple text and supportive images introduce beginning readers to the physical characteristics and geographic locations of deserts."
  Includes bibliographical references and index.
  ISBN-10: 1-60014-035-1 (hardcover : alk. paper)
  ISBN-13: 978-1-60014-035-8 (hardcover : alk. paper)
  1. Deserts—Juvenile literature. I. Title. II. Series.

GB612.G74 2007
551.41'5–dc22   2006000569

Text copyright © 2007 by Bellwether Media.
Printed in the United States of America.

Table of Contents

Deserts are the driest
places on Earth. Very little
rain falls in a desert.

The ground and the air are dry in the desert. When rain does fall, the water **evaporates** quickly.

Not all deserts are hot.
Some deserts are very cold.

Antarctica is the largest, driest, and coldest desert on Earth. Ice covers Antarctica all year.

7

Most deserts are hot. The **Sahara Desert** in Africa is the largest hot desert on Earth.

Rocks and sand cover most of the Sahara Desert.

The sun shines down on a hot desert during the day. There are few clouds to block the heat of the sun.

Most desert animals
hide during the day
to stay cool.

Hot deserts can be cold at night. There are few clouds to trap the daytime heat near the ground.

Many desert animals look for food at night.

Dry winds blow across deserts. The wind blows sand into hills called **dunes**.

Over time, wind wears away rock. Blowing sand made this **arch** in the rock.

Wind and sand shaped
these rocks.

A gust of wind can make a small tornado called a **dust devil**.

Water lies deep under the ground in some deserts. A place where the water comes to the surface is called an **oasis**.

Desert animals drink water at an oasis. People can find water at an oasis.

Desert plants go for weeks
without water. A burst of
rain falls at last.

The plants bloom and make seeds. The rain brings new life to the desert.

Glossary

Antarctica—the continent that covers the South Pole; it is the largest, driest, and coldest desert on Earth.

arch—a curved shape with a hole under the curve

dunes—a shape that sand makes it when it is blown by the wind

dust devil—a small tornado in a desert or other hot, dry place

evaporate—to change from a liquid into a gas

oasis—a place in the desert where water comes up from underground streams

Sahara Desert—the largest hot desert on Earth

To Learn More

AT THE LIBRARY

Dunphy, Madeleine. *Here Is the Southwestern Desert*. New York: Hyperion Books, 1995.

Longenecker, Theresa. *Who Grows Up In the Desert?* Minneapolis, Minn. Picture Window Books, 2003.

Lowell, Susan. *The Tortoise and the Jackrabbit*. Flagstaff, Ariz. Northland, 1994.

Ward, Jennifer. *Way Out in the Desert*. Flagstaff, Ariz. Rising Moon, 1998.

ON THE WEB

Learning more about deserts is as easy as 1, 2, 3.

1. Go to www.factsurfer.com

2. Enter "deserts" into search box.

3. Click the "Surf" button and you will see a list of related web sites.

With factsurfer.com, finding more information is just a click away.

Index

The photographs in this book are reproduced through the courtesy of: Dennis Flaherty/Getty Images, front cover; Frans Lemmens/Getty Images, pp. 4-5, 8-9, 11, 18-19; Roger Mear/Getty Images, p. 6-7; Stephen Alvarez/Getty Images, p. 10; Orion Press/Getty Images, p. 12; Steve Maxlowski/Getty Images, p. 13; Sergio Pitamitz/Getty Images, p. 14; Laura Ciapponi/Getty Images, p. 15; Mark Newman/Getty Images, p. 16; Joel Sartore/Getty Images, p. 17; William Lesch/Getty Images, p. 20; VEER Christopher Talbot Frank/Getty Images, p. 21.